29 KEYS
TO PARENTING AND WIN!

Helping Your Children to . . .
Stay Out of Trouble . . .
Excel in School . . .
and Become Amazing Adults!!

LORENE PHILLIPS
A W EUGENE PHILLIPS

authorHOUSE®

AuthorHouse™ UK
1663 Liberty Drive
Bloomington, IN 47403 USA
www.authorhouse.co.uk
Phone: 0800.197.4150

Published by AuthorHouse 01/08/2018

ISBN: 978-1-5462-8230-3 (sc)
ISBN: 978-1-5462-8207-5 (e)

Print information available on the last page.

Contents

Foreword:

"Good parents want their kids to stay out of trouble, do well in school, and go on and do awesome things as an adult…" (Rachel Gillett and Drake Baer article, April 15, 2017).

Psychological research has confirmed what I think we already know: much of our children's success is based on a few things we need to do as parents. Yes, the buck stops with us as parents.

This book will serve as a reminder to parents that the quality of our children's upbringing is our primary responsibility. While other assistance can be provided through the school, the church or the community, ***the ultimate responsibility rests with us as parents to raise our children - period.*** We simply must do whatever we need to do in order to equip our children with the skills and values that enable them to win in life.

In the spirit of transparency, we have asked our 3 boys (**A**aron – 22 year old, university graduate and intern at a financial services company, aka Mr. Creative guy', **B**randon – our 18 year old middle son, athletic and aka 'Mr. Cool guy', and **Connor** - the baby of the family, 16 year old business minded entrepreneur, aka 'Mr. Confident' guy) to share with you their responses to 3 questions that you will undoubtedly find relatable.

1. **What does good parenting look like for you?**
   A – *A mutual relationship shared based on: respect, unconditional love, encouragement and the surety that you'll always be in an undoubtedly nurturing/safe environment.*
   B – *Someone who is always there for their child when they need them the most.*
   C – *When there is a good relationship they can be strict when appropriate and playful and share a laugh as well.*

2. **What one thing would you like your parents to do more of?**
   A – *I know my parents have my best interest at heart always, but I wish my parents would let me express myself fully before correcting me/providing their wisdom or insight. I know it's based on love, but it can come off as discouraging from the child's point of view.*
   B – *Be more relaxed with tough decisions.*
   C – *One thing that I would like my parents to do more of is continue to be motivational and believe in us, as it gives us a lot of confidence in our aspirations.*

3. **If you could tell your parents to stop doing one thing right away what would that be?**

A – *Tell them to stop worrying that I'm going to make a wrong decision/course of action. They have raised me in such a way that it is literally impossible for me to fail.*
(Also mum, could you do me a favor & and
bring back a knife set from IKEA?)
B – *Stop getting so angry.*
C – *One thing that I would tell my parents to stop being is over protective, as some lessons can and will be learned the hard way, and by being too protective it can lead to a child wanting to make the wrong decisions more.*

Introduction

Lorene:

I always knew I wanted to be a parent, but was uncertain of whether I would be any good at it. It was not an overwhelming fear, but it was most certainly a concern.

My own childhood was riddled with much dysfunctionality: generous helpings of abandonment, lack of validation, and rejection with one transition after the next. Stability and normalcy were a distant dream, and surviving was the driving force. Blessed with smarts, great people skills, and athletic abilities, I was able to overcompensate for these obvious failings and 'succeed'.

My relationship with God was by far the only part of my life that was true and sure. When you have not been parented in a healthy way, only encountering snippets of knowledge from various adults who popped in and out of your life as 'parents', it became very clear that I had no idea about the quality of parenting I would adopt in my own life, should I be blessed to be a mother. Would I be better than what was modeled before me, or would I be worse?

Parenting (like marriage), was the beginning of the undoing of my previous self. I discovered that parenting is by far the toughest, most challenging, self-revealing, humbling and vulnerable role I have ever been responsible for in my life. I chose to be a parent three times, and I am still in awe at what a unique and incredible honor it is to be given the opportunity to influence and love unconditionally another human being.

Once again, God has been faithful in providing me with a husband who loves me unconditionally, and who also extended this same love to our boys. I was able for the first time to experience the truth of godly parenting in partnership with a humble and loving husband. My husband and I made a commitment from the beginning that our marriage would be a priority, and that this will set the tone and priority for the raising of our children.

Our desire is to ultimately raise children who know that they are loved unconditionally and who understand that their purpose in life is to show Christ through their gifts and talents. Our children are our responsibility wholly and completely – *we do not delegate our authority or responsibility to anyone else, and we answer directly to God for how we parent them.* This ministry of parenting is a high calling, and we want to be faithful in this area of our lives so that our children and future generations will be blessed because of our decisions.

Introduction

Eugene:

As I sit and reflect on my life as a husband, father, brother and son; I realize that life is full of surprises, both exciting, unexpected, and, in a few cases, terrifying! Being a parent is an awesome blessing, we get to partner with the creator of the universe, and play a first-hand role in the molding of our children to become the people that they were created to become! Great! There's just one small caveat – our 'precious in the sight of God' gems don't come with customized manuals at birth – or do they? I believe they do, it's just that we must understand the 'manual' before we can apply it, and know ahead of their birth that there is a customized manual available now.

There's a verse in this manual, Ephesians 2:10, that pretty much sums it up for us.

10 For we are God's [own] handiwork (His workmanship), ᵍrecreated in Christ Jesus, [born anew] that we may do those good works which God predestined (planned beforehand) for us [taking paths which He prepared ahead of time],

that we should walk in them [living the good life which He prearranged and made ready for us to live].

g Arthur S. Way, *Way's Epistles: The Letters of St. Paul to Seven Churches and Three Friends.*

The Amplified Bible. (1987). (Eph 2:10). La Habra, CA: The Lockman Foundation.

We (including our children), are God's handiwork and He made provision for us through Christ - works that were prepared just for us individually, even custom made, we simply walk in them and they fit perfectly. So, **the blueprint for our children has already been written, we must simply follow it.**

As I reflect on how I was parented as an only child for 12 years, and then as a sibling to my younger brother, my parenting requirements were very different as Lorene and I became parents of three young boys all within a seven year span. Even though my parents' requirements were different, there were similarities as well. Lorene and I together were able to weigh our experience, and those of our parents, against the manual and/or apply those things that were consistent with God's design for parenting our children.

Your parenting requirements will be different than ours, as is to be expected, however if you build on God's Word as the foundation along with your own experiences, you will create the deliberate plan for parenting your children.

By no means are we experts, let's face it; I only have 22 years' experience! That being said, God is eternal, and He has no beginning or end. In fact HE is the first parent and is therefore qualified to 'recommend' how we should parent our children - to me that is a win!

Our aim here is to simply through transparency, share with you the ups and downs of our parenting, and share what we've learned along the way in the hope that it can be of help to you as you take this journey called parenting, and win!

29 KEYS

1

OBEDIENCE

– The primary responsibility of our children

Children, obey your parents in the Lord: for this is right -
Ephesians 6:1 *(KJV)*

The degree to which our children obey us in their early years sets the tone for the quality and effectiveness of our parenting as they develop into adults. This is the one commandment that is given specifically to children with a wonderful promised attached – one of a good quality life. So apart from making our lives easier as parents, obedience is the secret ingredient that allows our children to have the lives that we desire for them, a life which pleases God. They will be set up to work under authority, and be able to be obedient to the voice of God as they develop their own relationship with Christ.

APPLICATION:

I. *Can you think of one way you can help your child(ren) to start learning how to be obedient?*
II. *What behavior do you need to change as a parent that will help to create and support an environment for obedience?*

2

WORK ETHIC
– The importance of chores

Diligent hands will rule …. Proverbs 12:24; *All hard work brings a profit, but mere talk leads only to poverty* - Proverbs 14:23. (NKJV)

Chores are by far the best way to teach and train your children to develop among other things, the following core set of values:

- Work Ethic
- Responsibility
- Dependability
- Citizenship
- Team work
- Sense of contribution and achievement
- Confidence and self-esteem

The earlier you start the better it will be for your child(ren) and for your family. It is important that your list of chores are reflective of where each child is developmentally, e.g. a toddler may be required to put his shoes in the basket by the door, while a young child may be required to put his/her shoes on the shoe rack; a 6 year old may be asked to collect all the small trash bins and replace all trash bags, while your 12 year old may be asked to take the trash out for collection day, and return the trash bin at the end of the day.

There are so many online tools that can help you put together a chore list, and determine a reward system. In our home, we believe that chores are a key way in which our children can contribute at home, and we reserve any payment for exceptional efforts or initiative to take on special projects, like helping to organize the kitchen pantry, clean-up the garage or help to paint our retaining wall.

I cannot stress how important a role chores play in developing our children to be productive citizens, with a great sense of ambition and outlook on life. They develop skills such as perseverance, working with integrity, strong organizational skills, working well with others, maintaining focus on a task until it's satisfactorily completed, and experiencing the results that come from hard work – success. By honing these transferable skills early, these traits will serve to set our children apart when they enter the 'real world', and position them with confidence to take advantage of *any* opportunity presented to them.

I should also add that the benefit to parents is that it makes our lives much easier – with the children helping, the load is lighter for mom and dad. And we know that in a world where both parents often work or where the home is headed by a single parent, the joy of having this extra help frees us up to do some fun things with the kids, or just catch our breath!

I have copied below one of the chores list that we devised for our youngest child when he was 5 years old which could provide you some inspiration. Otherwise, do a search on the internet and look for other ideas and tips that can help to get you started in making chores at home an integral part of how your family functions.

If you are new to this, then I would suggest that you make sure to sit your children down and explain to them *what* the upcoming change will be, *why* you will be starting a chore list, and *how* the chore list will be designed. By all means, invite them to propose any ideas they may have. You are ultimately responsible for finalizing and executing this chore list, and in no time you will all start to reap the benefits.

We were not perfect in everything we did, and we were constantly tweaking and adjusting to make sure that the core values we wanted to achieve were at the center of the chore list. This is the real motivation for doing this in the first place. It takes a lot of time to properly execute, but it becomes easier as time goes by with everyone learning by trial and error, and everyone understanding the expectation level around each task. I assure you this is time well spent, and you will see the evidence of this lived out positively in your children's lives on a daily basis for the rest of their lives. Just take a second and think about what your children's lives could look like WITHOUT these core values – I don't believe this is what we desire for our children.

How can you start making chores in your home an intentional way to develop our children's character? I have listed a couple of questions in the application section below that you can consider acting on soonest.

APPLICATION:

I. *Think of 2 practical things that your child(ren) can start doing right away that can remove some of the pressure at home? How about little 5-year-old Amelia setting the table, her nine year old brother Cameron packing away the dishes, and Seven year old Jaimie setting up the table for breakfast tomorrow? You get the idea …. What ideas can you come up with? Solicit the kids and see what ideas they may have.*

II. *Set a date when you can complete a chore list for your kids and outline the steps to get it done.*

III. *Is there an App or some other tool that you could use to assist you with developing your chore list?*

IV. *Discuss with your spouse/partner how you will approach rewards around these chores – will it be for daily chores or more for special projects etc.?*

I hope that this section will prompt you to do something about making chores an intentional tool that you can use right away to help your children become the very best they can be, while helping YOU as parents be less stressed, freeing up some time to do fun things with your children. Now that's a happy home.

As I mentioned above, here is the chore list for our youngest when he was 5 years old (many years ago), that was posted in his room, bathroom and in the kitchen – and he also had a copy on a clip board that we would check and sign-off at the end of each day (great way to teach accountability!). Listen, it does not have to be perfect - the most important thing is that you start.

MORNINGS:

Make Bed --

Brush Teeth/Wash Face --

Get dressed --

Eat Breakfast: ---

School Bags & Jacket ---

EVENINGS:

Clean Lunchbox ---

Practice Music --

Organize uniform/Bag for next day --------------------------

Shower ---

TRASH   **Mon.** ---------   **Show 'N' Tell** ---------------

** **Pick up all toys as needed** **

3

FRIENDSHIPS
– Cultivating healthy relationships

Do not be misled: 'Bad company corrupts good character'
1 Corinthians 15:33 (NIV)

Wounds from a friend can be trusted, but an enemy multiplies kisses. - Proverbs 27:6 (NIV)

'Show me your company and I will tell you who you are'

How many times growing up was I warned, 'show me your company and I will tell you who you are'? It is crucial that we teach our children the value of good friendships, and more importantly, how they can be a good friend.

It is important that you discuss with your children in specific ways what a healthy friendship looks like, and equally important, what attributes make up an unhealthy relationship. Be specific and share with them appropriate examples from your past. This type of transparency builds trust, and is an opportunity to share a part of yourself with your children.

It is important that you pay keen attention to the friends your children spend a lot of time with, or that have a significant impact or influence on your children's behavior or choices.

Whilst it is important that our children form friendships, it is vitally important that we teach them how to choose wisely the friendships that will help them grow into fine adults, and which will enrich their lives with connections and joy, and last a lifetime.

So, make the effort to create a space in your home where your children's friends would love to be, and a home where you get an opportunity to also invest in the lives of their friends.

APPLICATION:

I.   *How can you make your home a place where your children's friends want to hang out?*

II. *Can you think of an opportunity to discuss with your children the characteristics of a good friend?*

III. *Can you share an example from your life where you made some poor choices in friends?*

4

SOCIAL MEDIA/INTERNET
– The things of the Internet

Above all else, guard your heart, for everything you do flows from it. Proverbs 4:23 (NIV)

23 *All things are lawful [that is, morally legitimate, permissible], but not all things are beneficial or advantageous. All things are lawful, but not all things are constructive [to character] and edifying [to spiritual life]. (AMP)*

24 *Don't be concerned for your own good but for the good of others. (NLT)*
1 Corinth. 10:23,24

"The institutions of American culture are changing, and the family is no exception. Forces like technology are influencing habits in the home and disrupting traditional norms that have shaped young people for generations. But some things never change—like the parental responsibility for setting and communicating the values of their home and family".

"Forming Family Values in a Digital Age - Infographics in Culture & Media • June 27, 2017, (https://www.barna.com/ research/forming-family-values-digital-age/) The Barna Group

Technology has become an integral part of everyday life. Self-parking/driving cars, connected refrigerators that order milk or eggs automatically when your supply is low, e-tickets, Apple pay, Sonos audio systems - the list goes on. I am a huge fan of technology and have made and enjoyed a fulfilling career in the technology space. One of the by-products of technology is Social Media:

- Facebook
- Whatsapp

- Snapchat
- Twitter
- Instagram
- LinkedIn, etc...

Social media is an amazing tool which allows you to easily keep in contact with friends and loved ones. Many corporations have also adopted social media as a differentiator between themselves and competitors with great success. Social media has been a game changer in both business, and on a personal level. It has changed the way we think, speak and, in many cases, act.

With this in mind as a parent, just because social media is available and free it does not mean that we should let our guards down and throw our children into the deep blue sea before they can swim. 1 Corinthians 10:24 – the apostle Paul is reminding us that we do not just have responsibility for ourselves, and we should consider whether any decision or action that we make or do may have a negative impact upon others. Some of the negative impacts of social media include, among others:

- Hate speech
- Cyber bullying
- Social distrust
- Identity theft
- False validation
- Explicit or violent imagery
- Online stalking/grooming

- Damage
- Lack of social skills

What I am essentially speaking about here is **perspective**. Having the right perspective is the difference between light and darkness. Social media in and off itself is not wholly negative, as we would all agree it is a powerful tool. It is our use and understanding of this tool which can be incorrect. Perhaps this is a good lead into asking and analyzing how we as parents use social media, and determine whether or not we are modelling the right perspective.

Our primary responsibility as parents is to love, nurture and protect our children as they grow so that they can develop into mature, responsible members of society. The answer or antidote for the drug called social media, is found in the right perspective. We must know who our children truly are, and who we see them to be when they are grown at 21 years old and set this as our goal. Once we understand this, we will then know how to handle the different stages in their lives and the major challenges that they may face. Social media can either be a major challenge, or another tool which we can introduce to our children, who can then go on and use them responsibly, rather than allowing social media to change who they are and impact what they think, say, or do.

Restated – analyze/understand firstly how you use social media (be honest now), Understand who your children are, and who you see them to be at age 21 (right perspective) and how you will shape /help them reach this goal. Social media only has the destructive power that we give to it.

APPLICATION:

I. *Pray – There are so many distractions and devices and systems bent on destroying our children, but we must remember we have a weapon - one that is far greater, smarter than any device known to man! Our Sovereign God is able to remove any obstacle or challenge our children face. In fact, He can also remove them completely without our children ever having to face them.*

II. *I've included a useful link from a CNN article that helps parents understand what is at stake when their children are on social media. It is very useful and also provides suggestions how to protect your children practically. http://edition.cnn.com/2016/01/25/health/ social-media-red-flags-for-parents/index.html*

III. *Sit down with your children and first understand how they are using the internet/social media, and answer any questions they may have.*

5

MONEY & FINANCIAL RESPONSIBILITY
– Teach good financial stewardship

...the LOVE of money is the root of all kinds of evil. 1 Timothy 6:10 (NIV); *... but whoever gathers money little by little makes it grow.* Proverbs 13:11 (NIV)

Managing money well is a skill we need to teach our children as early as possible. Being a great steward of your money will set your children up to succeed financially, and to live a financially responsible life, enabling them to achieve the things that are important to them.

When our children were younger, we taught them about splitting any money given to them into the following 3 categories or jars: GIVE, SAVE and SPEND. We discussed with them why it's important to think about your money in this way, and how to manage it well. Show them how to set up a basic budget, and how to track their spending. Find ways that work for your children.

As parents, we get an opportunity every day to show our children how we manage our finances. For example, buying what you can afford, staying away from debt, learning how to live on cash flow, and waiting for the things we need. Teaching your kids the difference between 'needs' and 'wants' is crucial.

As kids get older, along with the chores at home, you should encourage them to look for an opportunity to find a job, so they can start managing their own money. This makes for a great learning opportunity while at home. Don't be afraid to allow them to make wrong decisions at this stage, and experience the consequences of a lack of money.

Above all, teach them the heart of God concerning money and material possession. Help them to understand that their value and worth is not tied to the money they possess, but in the character of who they are. Help them find ways they can give back and influence the world. Show them how, when used wisely, money can accomplish great things through Christ. Money is just a tool and a resource that God has given us. He owns everything, and we are to be good stewards, acting with humility and a sense of gratitude and responsibility in order to use it to bless others.

APPLICATION:

I.   *How can you help your children understand how to spend their money?*

II. *Look for opportunities to show your children how you manage your finances such as budgeting for groceries etc.*

III. *When you tell your children 'no' to a purchase, make sure you take the time to explain why.*

IV. *Do your children understand the difference between a 'want' and a 'need'? If not, make sure you explain the difference.*

6

MANNERS
– Good etiquette prepares them to succeed

31 Do to others as you would have them do to you.
Luke 6:31 (NIV)

When our boys were young, we had, as a fixture on our table, a little book detailing manners for all situations. We would pick one and discuss it at the table. Such topics ranged from eating etiquette, to scenarios around social etiquettes as well as how to behave in public. We would also look for opportunities to specifically help our kids to use these skills outside the home. This would include teaching them how to order food at a restaurant, how to respectfully communicate to the waiter if something is wrong with the order, and the importance of saying thank you and leaving a tip.

Whenever we hosted parties at our home, the boys would be in full service from welcoming guests and hanging their coats etcetera, to assisting with parking and showing guests the facilities, and generally being available to answer any questions they may have. We empowered our kids to serve and help us in this way. Of course, from a practical perspective, this was a great help, but more importantly, an opportunity for them to hone their social skills. Soon, they became proficient in these areas, and could introduce themselves and be at ease around different people, all the while being confident and well mannered.

These skills matter, and as parents we must be particularly mindful to teach and expose our children to the right opportunities in order for them to excel in this area. It won't be long before you start to see the difference this makes in their social interactions and confidence level.

APPLICATION:

I.   *Make a dinner reservation at a family restaurant and give your family an opportunity to practice their table manners and 'please' and thank you'.*

II. *Start making setting the table a priority so your children become comfortable with using the cutleries, and accustomed to asking to be excused from the table etc.*

III. *Devise a reward system for recognizing good table manners.*

7

INTIMACY WITH GOD
– Helping our children to know God for themselves

John 17:3 And this is the way to have eternal life—to know you, the only true God, and Jesus Christ, the one you sent to earth. (LASBNLT)

… If anyone hears my voice and opens the door, I will come in and eat with that person and they with me. Revelation 3:20

Intimacy is a term which has been widely restricted to those activities of a sexual nature. The media is guilty through reality shows, movies and novels that portray intimacy on this level. Intimacy is much more than just that. The dictionary defines intimacy as "the state of being intimate". It further explains it as: "a close, familiar and usually affectionate or loving personal relationship with another person or group". We have a God who loves us, and by definition is infinite in His knowledge and understanding of us. He is familiar with us because He created us, and He desires this close relationship with each of us. This desire to have such a relationship is demonstrated in the verse quoted in Hosea 6:6, 'He considers dutiful steadfast love and goodness', and then in John 17:3, 'the only way to eternal life is to **_know_** God (intimacy) through Jesus Christ'.

Close relationships are part of God's will for human life. How do we help our children to know God for themselves on this level? We mirror the same action and character of God when we parent our children. We provide opportunity for them to know us, and this allows them to know God intimately when they make that decision to follow Christ. I am convinced that if we do not allow, foster and promote intimacy in our homes, we hinder our children from truly knowing Jesus to the fullest as He wants them to. One of the greatest indictments against men has been the drive to suppress our feelings because to express them is not manly. Intimacy is best nurtured in a safe home environment, where family can together navigate through triumphs, difficult times, pain and celebration! Establish trust with your children, and do not be afraid to allow them to share in some of your struggles and hurts. Let them see your intimacy with Christ through all types of life situations. Let them see you talking with Jesus you are demonstrating how you have intimacy with God.

APPLICATION:

I. *The next time you experience difficulty – where appropriate, speak with your children in terms they understand, and let them know how you feel, and what you are doing to navigate through the problem or situation. You are inviting them into your life by being transparent and potentially vulnerable – great training ground!*

II. *Who do you consider a true friend, someone with whom you can be transparent?*

8

AUTHORITY
– Learning HOW to serve others well

Do nothing out of selfish ambition or vain conceit. Rather in humility value others above yourself. Phil 2:3 (NIV)

Home is the best place to teach this skill. As parents, we are the authority in our home, under God. We communicate this structure very early and regularly to our children, and ensure that they understand that this is done in an environment of unconditional love. It may not be perfect all the time, and that's ok as long as they understand the buck stops with us, and that we answer to God for all that we do.

By getting involved in serving each other as family members, whether that be in tasks such as setting the table, helping to make a meal, folding the laundry or helping with landscaping the family's lawn etc., we allow our children to understand what proper authority looks like. By teaching our children to serve well at home, we ensure they will be able to successfully serve others well in their school, in their community and in life.

APPLICATION:

I.   *What is preventing you from asking your children How are you demonstrating a servant leader attitude to your children?*

II. *Do your children understand by your words and your actions that you are the respectful authority in your home?*

9

COURAGE AND RESILIENCE
– The difference between a setback and a failure

When I am afraid I put my trust in you ...Psalm 56:3 (NIV)

The battle is won when we keep getting up – Mandisa "Out of the Dark, Keep Getting Up."

How do we develop the trait of courage and resilience in our children? – by giving them the opportunity to try new things and fail. The earlier you do this, the better able our children will be in understanding that failing at something does not make them a failure, and neither does it define them. Instead, failing teaches you what not to do or what to do differently the next time, so that they have a better chance of succeeding. Sports were a great tool in teaching our kids these life lessons in the early years. But, as they became older and experienced new failures in relationships, school and life, we had to adapt our strategies, and be there to help them through those times, and to affirm their values as individuals. We use these tough times to remind them that what we do is not who we are, and that God has a good plan for their lives – a plan that was set out before they were conceived. (*Ephesians 2:10*)

Our children must learn that they are not a failure because they failed, and that their value is in the character of who they are. This belief will compel them to keep trying, and will help to build the courage and resilience that they will require to succeed in life.

APPLICATION:

I. *Next time your child experiences a loss, have a plan on how you will acknowledge the learning experience.*

II. *How can you help your child to show grace next time he/she suffers a loss?*

III. *What one thing do you need to change as a parent to help your child(ren) become stronger after experiencing a setback?*

10

TRYING NEW THINGS
– Keeps life exciting and fresh

Take moments & memories over possessions. Unknown

Look for opportunities to expose your children to new people, places and experiences. Help them to discover how multifaceted and complex they are as human beings. Expose them to the world and the joy and pain of humanity. Help them to develop compassion and empathy for others. Foster in them a desire to understand others that may be different from them, and affirm through these differences how valuable they are, and the awesome purpose they play in this game that is life.

We relocated from our home when the boys were teenagers, and despite initial concerns, we were courageous enough as a family to dare ourselves to have new experiences as individuals, and together as a family. Money cannot buy the invaluable lessons and growth we experienced because of this decision. We became closer as a family, more adventurous and tolerant of others. We travelled as much as we could, and we saw our boys become independent and responsible as young men – fully capable of taking care of themselves. We are extremely proud of being brave enough to allow our children to experience first-hand the joy a new way of life can bring.

APPLICATION:

I. *What one experience would you love to do as a family that you have not yet done? Now do some research, and make plans.*

II. *Can you think of an activity you can do together that does not cost any money? Get your kids involved, and make a list of their suggestions*

III. *Can you think of an activity you did as a kid, such as fishing, hiking, playing board games, tennis or basketball etc. How can you introduce your kids to these activities, and create new memories while sharing your own childhood memories with your family?*

11

CHOICES
– The way to empower our children

…So, chose life in order that you may live, you and your descendants. Deuteronomy 30:19

Life is a matter of choices, and every choice you make makes you. John Maxwell

Teaching your children about the power of choice is uplifting. It is important that they understand that they were created to choose right from wrong, and to be responsible for the outcome of those choices. We have made a concerted effort to look for opportunities to help our children think for themselves, and begin to learn how to make age appropriate decisions. This was particularly difficult to do when we knew they were not the best decisions, but we understood that the long-term goal was to teach them how to make better choices when the stakes are low, so that in later years when the stakes are higher, they will be ready to apply the same principles and make better decisions.

When we create an environment for our children that allows them to make choices, and experience the consequences of those decisions, they are able to learn. This is an opportunity for us to either show grace, establish boundaries or affirm with rewards.

APPLICATION:

I.   *Can you think of an opportunity to help your children learn the benefits and consequences of choices while at home?*

II. *How can you support your children in making good choices?*

III. *Do you have a plan in place to deal with situations when your children make bad choices? If you do not have one, start considering the various scenarios and associated consequences*

12

INVESTING TIME
– Understanding the season of parenting effectively

Spend time with those you love. One of these days you will say either 'I wish I had' or 'I'm glad I did'. (Unknown)

'When in doubt choose the kids. There will be plenty of time later to choose work'. (Unknown)

Our overall goal is that our children may be growing in love for God and others as they grow in submission to the lordship of Christ. Stephen J. Cole

Parenting is a gift of time that we should use mindfully. If we do not, the true meaning of our role will get gobbled up by competing priorities (especially good ones), routine, chaos, hurriedness and the weight of responsibility and striving. We must be mindful that we are responsible for developing in our children character, meaning and purpose, proper perspective, and a great example of living life honestly, despite all its flaws.

What type of person do you dream of your kids becoming? Start making decisions right now that will help to develop that 2-year-old into the awesome young man or woman that you desire. We must adopt a long-term perspective when it comes to parenting, so we can make the best decisions for our children's lives. This mindset will help us to hold the line, especially when we must make those difficult decisions that our children do not like, causing them to think of us as the worst parents in the world.

Our task is to simply love our children unconditionally, and help them develop the gifts that God has given them. We should look for opportunities to create great memories, and close bonds that will last for years to come.

APPLICATION:

I. *What one thing can you change that can create time for your family and communicate to them that they are a priority?*

II. *Ask your children to tell you what they value in you as a parent that already communicates love to them. Ask them if there is anything else that they desire from you that would communicates love to them.*

13

PRIORITISING PARENTING
– Making parenting intentional

Attention, Israel! GOD, our God! GOD the one and only! Love GOD, your God, with your whole heart: love him with all that's in you, love him with all you've got! Write these commandments that I've given you today on your hearts. Get them inside of you and then get them inside your children. Talk about them

wherever you are, sitting at home or walking in the street; talk about them from the time you get up in the morning to when you fall into bed at night. Tie them on your hands and foreheads as a reminder; inscribe them on the doorposts of your homes and on your city gates.

Peterson, E. H. (2005). The Message: the Bible in contemporary language (Dt 6:4–9). Colorado Springs, CO: NavPress.

Realizing that our children are gifts from God, and that we were specifically chosen to parent them as our top priority is key to establishing a firm foundation with which we build on throughout their lives. Lorene and I learned this early in our parenting. I can remember clearly the moment when we realized this important key – Prioritized Parenting. As young professionals, we were purely focused on our jobs, working hard to provide for our family. We were blessed with an amazing support network of grandparents, aunts, uncles and close friends. So, we could work extra hours, leave the kids with family if they were sick, and coordinate pickups as needed. We had the system down pat, our immediate family group were excited to assist, and were reliable and such a blessing. (*Pause, 'pat of the back' sigh*) We were 'great parents', or, at least we thought we had this parenting thing down…

It was a beautiful day, and Lorene and I were busy establishing our careers, providing for the family, and then the call came – our prearranged pickup driver was unable to collect Aaron, where he was waiting at the opposite end of the island (Bermuda). Immediately, we began taking turns contacting our amazing support network, but with no success! Can you believe the nerve of our family not being available for my son, what else are they doing? Nothing is more important than my son! Then, as clear as day I heard the still, small voice of the Lord speaking .…. but he is **_YOUR_** son..! This was the moment I knew I had to make parenting a priority – not just the big easy stuff, but just as important, the smaller stuff. My children are just that, *my* children – family support is just support, not the first line of support, but the fallback support. It is all about perspective. In my situation, it was not the fault of the family member or friend that they were unavailable for what I needed; I must be the first line of support for my children. From that day, we made this aspect of parenting a priority, and made the necessary adjustments to our work routine, including setting the expectation with our respective bosses concerning pickups in the event of emergencies. We scheduled ourselves as first line responsibility in this area, with family and friend's secondary. So, if we have to stop work for a pickup because a pre-organized pickup has fallen through, we do just that, because our children are our number 1 priority.

APPLICATION

I. *Consider work, social and family life - Write down those things that are priority in your life - where do the children factor?*

II. *Start small – instead of organizing a pickup – you do the pickup instead.*

14

SPORTS AND OTHER ACTIVITIES
— Teaching life lessons through extracurricular activities

"Do you not know that in a race all the runners compete, but [only] one receives the prize? o run [your race] that you may lay hold [of the prize] and make it yours."
1 Corinth 9:24 AMP

"Sports do not build character. They reveal it." Heywood Broun

Get involved with their sports and other activities, even if you're not good at it! Make room for them in this area. Find a sport or activity that your son or daughter enjoys or has an aptitude for, and get involved with them in that sport or activity. Whether it is as a spectator (greatest cheerleader) or as a coach, do it together.

I love most sports, both playing and watching. Growing up I was involved with baseball, and played lots of it. As an adult, even before children, I got involved in Little League Baseball (coaching and volunteering). A Cal Ripken Baseball certificate later, I was coaching Little League and, might I say, wasn't bad at it at all. I love baseball because, a) my grandfather and I would watch it all the time, b) I love the strategy of the game, and, c) there are lots of life lessons learned through baseball or sports/activities in general. To name a few, how to follow rules, work as a team, make your daddy happy (*how'd that one get in there*). Sports and other activities teach our children the benefits of hard work, perseverance, goal setting, individual development whilst contributing within a team environment, and how to win with integrity. There are many rule adjustments added to the youth game which make sense, but there was one rule which, if made official, would totally reverse an important life lesson. It is the principle of rewarding everyone just for showing up. In the game of baseball, we play to win with integrity, not to demean the opponent (that's why they have the mercy rule). We don't play to give everyone a trophy just because they drove to the field. That's why we have most improved or coach's player of the season awards. If we establish this rule, then we are positioning our children to expect a reward for little to no work produced. How does that work in the real world? It doesn't – in the workplace we are promoted if we perform well, if we don't we are not rewarded, and in cases often, we may be transferred or released. To learn these life lessons when we are young is much better than learning this as an adult. Children are far more resilient than adults in situations like these. Getting involved as parents allows us to be there for them when they lose, encourage and guide them through this. We help them to realize that loss is not failure, but a teaching opportunity and, most importantly, to know that our God is Sovereign, and even when we lose a baseball game, we are still winners at baseball!

APPLICATION:

I. *Find out what activities your children enjoy, and participate with them (spectator, volunteer or coach).*
II. *When participating in sports or extracurricular activities – embrace the competition without devaluing another human being. Show your children how to win and lose well.*

15

HELPING OTHERS
– Humility to serve others

*Humble yourselves before the Lord and he will
lift you up in honor.* James 4:10 (NLT)

Raising children who have an attitude to serve others with
humility is a character trait that we should strive to develop as
soon as is possible. Either working with a charity organization,
helping at church, or in the community, will help our
children to develop this. It teaches them to be selfless, and
to be motivated by doing good for others with nothing in it
for themselves. They will experience first-hand the amazing
feeling of achievement from using their talent and skills for
the sole purpose of helping others. After all, we want to be
a part of helping our children to become young men and
women who will contribute to and participate in adding value
to their families, communities and country.

APPLICATION:

I. *Find a volunteer activity that your children can participate in for the sole purpose of helping others.*

II. *Help your children to identify toys or clothing they no longer require that is in great condition and donate it to a charity. Get them to organize the items and participate in delivering them to the charity organizations.*

16

RESPECT

– Knowing how to give and receive respect

Show respect for all men [treat them honorably]... 1 Peter 2:17 (AMP)

Be a good citizen. All governments are under God. Insofar as there is peace and order, it's God's order. So live responsibly as a citizen. If you're irresponsible to the state, then you're irresponsible with God, and God will hold you responsible. Duly constituted authorities are only a threat if you're trying to get by with something. Decent citizens should have nothing to fear. Peterson, E. H. (2005). The Message: the Bible in contemporary language (Ro 13:1–3). Colorado Springs, CO: NavPress.

'Respect your Elders!'

I remember growing up as a child and always hearing the phrase, 'respect your elders!' This was the standard response used whenever my parents or other adults either didn't know the answer, or were not inclined to go any further with the discussion because they were tired (it had been a long day). Of course, it was used legitimately when I was out of line and a bit too familiar. This familiarity was always accompanied with the rhetorical question, 'Did we play marbles together as kids?' and, on occasion, a 'loving' tap when warranted. Of course, I was the perfect child, and the 'loving tap' was never needed. I remember thinking – 'I can't wait until I am an adult and I can say 'respect your elders!'. I got my chance, but it didn't have the affect I thought it would.

Fast forward to today, and the concept of respect has evolved into far more than 'respect your elders'. Today, the term 'respect' is often used as the evidence needed to harm another person or support bad behaviour. Gangs often quote the reason for committing horrible crimes as disrespect. Usually in this case, respect is required but never given. To take someone's life, or to humiliate another human being is not respect, it's the opposite, disrespect. How did we get here?

Respect is earned, and not an entitlement.

When parenting the boys, we always looked for opportunities to allow them to earn our respect. We made sure to let them know that we respected them e.g. for sticking up for their brothers or a cousin at school or camp (loyalty), or helping out when not asked to because it was the right thing to do (integrity). The key here is to verbalize your respect for them as they learn the term, whilst at the same time understanding what action caused the respect. That's the key – as for children affirmation is best served audibly at first.

The key here as we parent, is that if our children are disrespectful to you or others, they won't be respectful to God at all.

APPLICATION:

I. *The next time the children are fighting over wearing each other's clothing, make the time to engage in conversation about respecting each other's property.*

II. *Set boundaries for yourself as a parent – for example, when daddy is reading I ask that you respect my time to allow me to read.*

III. *During the next crisis when one sibling may be hurt or sad, engage the other sibling to support his or her brother or sister by showing respect for their feelings.*

17

MANHOOD / WOMANHOOD
– Maturing & developing character

When I was a child, I talked like a child, I thought like a child, I reasoned like a child. When I became a man, I put the ways of childhood behind me. 1 Corinthians 13:11 (NIV)

I remember always wanting to be like my father and grandfather when I grew up. These were people whom I greatly respected as I watched in awe how they lived their lives, and the accomplishments they achieved. I remember enjoying the things they enjoyed, because it made me feel like I was like them. It wasn't until their funeral services, that I learned the fullness of their character through the large attendance at each of the services, and by the numerous words of comfort and experiences shared in reference to each of them. Words like integrity, dependability, authenticity and loving. Many lives were impacted for good because of their individual characters. They were friends for life – people would give all of themselves if either had asked. This was, for me, the evidence of those experiences I had as a child, spending my time in awe of both my father, and my grandfather. They became the models that I wanted my children to embrace and become. But, for the boys, they sadly did not have the pleasure of knowing my father or grandfather. However, they had me, and through my knowledge of these great men, I knew I must be the one to teach and nurture them in this area. You see, my grandfather and father fashioned their lives on two principles, 1) Love the Lord with all your heart, mind body and soul, and, 2) love your neighbor as yourself.

As we parent in this area, we too should firstly govern ourselves on the same principles, and then work this out with our children by spending time with them, and being there when they need to make a decision - no matter how small we think they are (remember, "when I was a child, I thought like a child…" 1 Corinth 13:11 (NIV)). This method gives us the awesome joy of molding the same principles in our children through real-life relevant situations, which of course change as they grow and mature – remember that the situations may change, but the result is the same!

🗝 APPLICATION:

I. *Begin to include your children when securing the house at night, making sure the doors are locked, or cleaning up the kitchen when it is not your turn to do the chores. This transitions our children to begin thinking more of what we do because it needs to be done, rather than it being their turn.*

II. *What decisions are you facing today concerning your children? Is it something you can discuss with them now? If so, involve them and facilitate making the decision with their input.*

18

MODELING

– Our actions reveal who we really are

"Children are great imitators. So, give them something great to imitate." (Unknown)

It's not a surprise that our children will learn more from what we do than what we say to them. As they get older and mature, becoming independent in their thinking, they will give us honest feed-back – whether we like it or not. Be mindful of the impact our decisions, ethics and lifestyle have on our children for the long-term. If you are casual in this area, you will live to see the negative impact that this attitude will have in their lives. It will create hurdles and unnecessary challenges that can serve to set our children behind, and short-circuit their chance to be successful in life. Remember, 'more is caught than taught'.

APPLICATION:

I. *Think of 2 areas that you are modelling well for your children?*

II. *In what areas are your words not consistent with your actions? Now what can you do right away to change that?*

19

RELATIONSHIPS

– The value of creating and maintaining loving relationships

"Treasure your relationships, not your possessions." Anthony J. D'Angelo

"Relationships never die a natural death. They are always murdered by attitude, behavior, ego or ignorance." (Unknown)

More and more I have become convinced that good quality relationships are the key to living a life that is balanced, fulfilling and meaningful. Great relationships make us happier because the human connection is what we were created for. Think about it – we are all more alike than we are different. We fundamentally care about the same things, and if we are fortunate enough to have healthy and amazing relationships, we consider ourselves blessed.

My childhood friends are still very much a part of my life; I work at my marriage to ensure that it remains healthy; and

I love spending time with family and friends, creating fun times and shared memories.

It is therefore important that we show our children how to develop healthy relationships with others by showing compassion, empathy, kindness, respect, forgiveness and so on. We desire for our children to have the richness of great relationships, so they can understand the joy of being a great friend or partner, and reap the benefit of that in their own lives.

⚷ APPLICATION:

I. *What can you do more of to stay connected to your friends?*
II. *Think of a friend that you really need to connect with. Make contact in the next 3 days.*

20

COMMUNICATION

– Learning how to understand and how to be understood

10% of conflict is due to difference in opinion and 90% is due to delivery & tone of voice.

"The most important thing in communication is hearing what isn't said." Dr. Peter F. Drucker

Helping our children to learn how to communicate is critical. This is a skill that will serve them well, especially when they need to articulate their concerns or frustrations in a productive way. We have 3 boys, and so we had to work particularly at this area. Conversations at the dinner table were great opportunities to hear them express themselves on contentious issues, and gave us an opportunity as parents to hear their views, and share ours. We get to challenge them, and see how they respond. We get the opportunity to hear how their minds work, and see their heart on various issues.

Good and honest communication allow our children to value the power of words, and to use it well, giving them the freedom to express themselves with honesty, responsibility and respect.

APPLICATION:

I.   *Consider how you can engage your children in an open dialogue about a topic of interest to them. Make sure you practice active listening during this time.*

II. *What one behavior can you change to encourage your children to communicate more honestly with you?*

21

IDENTITY
– The importance of knowing your worth

"Lord you are my identity And I know, I know... I know who I am." Israel Houghton song 'I know who I am'

A family structure plays a vital role in building worth in our children, or destroying it. The world out there is tough and unfair, and our children need a home where they are built up and prepared to interact with the world using resilience, confidence and courage.

Choose to deliberately speak positive and life building affirmations into our children's lives. Equally, seek out opportunities for them to learn how to be a better person, and help them to grow in those areas. Our responsibility is to love our children unconditionally, which includes setting appropriate boundaries, as we need to help them achieve their best potential. Yes, I am talking about tough love. Our children need to understand that we love them so much that we will not accept anything less than what we know they can achieve. We must take the time to know our children individually to be able to parent each child in a way that works for them. No 'cookie cutter' approach will work. They are each unique and one of a kind, with a separate path for their life. Let's raise the bar for our children to excel at home by being their greatest coach, advocate and cheerleader!

APPLICATION:

I. *Can you think of an activity that you can do together as a family that is fun, and offers a true opportunity for creating a sense of identity and belonging?*

II. *Look for opportunities to share with your children your own childhood memories.*

III. *What social event can you host at your home to facilitate new family traditions and celebrate old traditions?*

22

GOD'S SOVEREIGNTY
– The creator of the universe watches over you

Christ is the visible image of the invisible God. He existed before anything was created and is supreme over all creation. Colossians 1:15 (NLT)

...for through him God created everything in the heavenly realms and on earth. He made the things we can see and the things we can't see— such as thrones, kingdoms, rulers, and authorities in the unseen world. Everything was created through him and for him.
(Colossians 1:16) NLT

God is above all things and before all things. He is the alpha and the omega, the beginning and the end. He is immortal, and He is present everywhere so that everyone can know Him (Revelation 21:6).

How do we see the Sovereignty of God? By understanding that there is someone greater than the universe, someone who can't be beaten, and is not subject to time or space; by understanding that this same someone created all things, but is not subject to anything, and most importantly, someone who can do no wrong, has all the answers and is always there – that's when we fully understand the Sovereignty of God. God is Love, His Love is perfect and He loves you and me. It is this love that shines through His sovereignty and watches over us, always. This understanding is the very hope that we have as believers in Jesus Christ. It is the peace that we experience as we parent, even in the worst of parenting times, not what we feel, but what we know – hope, because we know that God is with us and that He can bring us and our children through! We can ask Him anything because He is always present everywhere (Omnipresent), He has unlimited authority and power (Omnipotent) and of infinite knowledge (Omniscient)! And it gets better because HE promises this:

We are assured and know that [God being a partner in their labor] all things work together and are [fitting into a plan] for good to and for those who love God and are called according to [His] design and purpose. The Amplified Bible. (1987). (Ro 8:28). La Habra, CA: The Lockman Foundation.

This very same promise, hope and peace, is what we want to pass onto our children.

I remember during one of the worst experiences I've ever been through in my life as a family, our faith was tested, but His Sovereignty and promise stood true – as a family we lived through this knowing that Sovereign God watches over us, and that He keeps His promises.

APPLICATION:

I. *As you prepare for your next family vacation, special event or day at work/school, use this opportunity to share with your children how you are trusting a Sovereign God who is watching over everything concerning your plans and activity.*

II. *Evaluate how you see God and His Sovereignty – have a clear understanding of what you believe in this area. What will allow you to see God in this way so that you will be able to nurture this in your child?*

23

BOUNDARIES & DISCIPLINE
– Establishing guardrails

No discipline is enjoyable while it is happening – it's painful. But afterward there will be a peaceful harvest of right living for those who are trained in this way. Hebrews 12:11 (NLT)

Discipline your child, and he will give you rest; he will bring you happiness. Proverbs 29:17

I was raised in a Caribbean culture, and so experienced the benefits and the pain (physical!) of discipline. When boundaries and discipline are carried out with love and consistency, our children will value them in later years - like we did. It is vital that we take a long-term view in this area. These boundaries will serve to save the very life of our children, and reduce the potential for long-term, harmful and destructive impact on their lives, and those of their children. The quality of children's lives will be better because a loving parent made the time to discipline effectively the child he loves so much, for the benefit of that child. You will see these boundaries serving to instill discipline and good decision making as our children mature.

APPLICATION:

I.   *If you get stressed out applying discipline when necessary, then start thinking now about some standard consequences you would deliver for infractions such as frequently forgetting items, keeping a messy room, poor attitude etc.*

II. *Reflect on how you were disciplined as a child. Is there one approach that you think could work for your family?*

III. *What is the long-term picture you have of your children? Start to think how consistently setting boundaries can help you achieve this goal.*

24

HEALTHY LIFESTYLE
– Taking care of our bodies is a loving act

...Honor God with your bodies. 1 Corinthians 6:20

The greatest wealth is health - Unknown

We try to show our children by example how to take care of their bodies, and to develop a lifestyle of discipline and moderation. By no means are we perfect in this area, but we are transparent and honest in communicating ways in which we can all do better as individuals and as a family.

It's important that food selection and preparation is reflective of a healthy lifestyle. Physical activities should play an important part of this healthy lifestyle.

This is crucial to our quality of life and that of our children, and for generations to come. If you need help in this area, get it. It's too important to ignore it. It's important that we are taught how to do this better, and help our children if necessary, get the help they may need in order to lead a physically healthy life. This will boost their confidence, and free them up to enjoy life in a healthy way.

APPLICATION:

I. *Think about an activity that you really enjoy and start incorporating that activity into your schedule.*

II. *Is there a friend (s) that you can invite to participate with you in improving the frequency of exercise, accountability and fun factor?*

25

INTEGRITY

– Developing consistency of character

The integrity of the upright guides them, but the unfaithful are destroyed by their duplicity. Proverbs 11:3 (NIV)

3 Receive instruction in wise dealing and the discipline of wise thoughtfulness, righteousness, justice, and integrity,

4 That prudence may be given to the simple, and knowledge, discretion, and discernment to the youth—

The Amplified Bible. (1987). (Pr 1:3–4). La Habra, CA: The Lockman Foundation.

Integrity is conforming reality to our words – in other words, keeping promises and expectations. Stephen Covey

Integrity is probably one of the hardest character traits to foster as an individual, let alone as a parent for your children to follow. The best definition of integrity in our everyday lives I learned from my mentor, and bible study teacher, Dr. Glen Bascome, and that is – ***"Integrity is doing what you are supposed to do(what is right) when no one is looking!"***. What a challenge! But, it has proven effective, because the only motivation for what we do in this scenario is what's in your heart, and not any pressure from those around you. Children understand this when told, as they can easily visualize doing something when no one else is around – that's the truest test for integrity.

But how do we know what is right? Simply stated, everything we do must be established on the foundation of Christ. It is the character of Christ that demands doing what is right at all times, and we simply have to follow. Easier said than done, especially in a world were *"whatever is 'right' for you is best"* or *"as long as you don't get caught"*. Lorene and I always use the Old Testament book of Proverbs as the integrity developer, because it teaches you (*especially young people*) "...how to live disciplined and successful lives, to help them do what is right, just and fair." Proverbs 1:3. The Book of Proverbs is such a great resource that we have continued to use them with our boys straight into their young adult years.

Be intentional in your looking for opportunities to put into practice those small chances to talk about the right response to situations, based on the wise lessons of Proverbs. For example, explaining why we don't break the speed limit on a straight open road when there is no one around to see us go as fast as we can!

APPLICATION:

I.   *Write down those traits that demonstrate integrity of character – discuss these traits with your children so that they understand, and then reinforce them when the opportunity arises, and mark my word – it will.*

II. *Highlight a biblical character with the kids – persons who demonstrate integrity and good character e.g. Daniel*

III. *Read a good book or watch a good movie, that highlight the traits that you want your children to develop – this is a great way to demonstrate visually to your children good character.*

26

FAITH

– Understanding the character of God = a Reasonable Faith

Now faith is the confidence in what we hope for and assurance about what we do not see. Hebrews 11:1 (NIV)

Faith is taking the first step even when you don't see the whole staircase. Martin Luther King Jr.

Christianity is not based on blind faith, but on informed understanding leading to ongoing trust. Stuart McAllister

Aaron, our firstborn, is so gifted, talented and naturally skilled at many things. He is also one who does not like to stand out from the crowd, even though he does so naturally because of his abilities. I remember when he was in primary school, Aaron was invited to play his violin in a school concert. This concert was in the main auditorium in Bermuda, in front of many parents and students from all over the island. Somehow, we did not get the memo and Aaron was decked out ⸪ in his school uniform, whilst the other participants were smartly dressed, but not in school uniform – well…. this was a catastrophic problem for Aaron! There was no way on this planet that Aaron was going to perform! He was not dressed appropriately (so he thought), and therefore would stand out - his absolute deal breaker! He would not budge! So, you can imagine what it was like back stage. I was able to finally get him to accompany me downstairs to the dressing room, where there was privacy, and he immediately began to listen whilst I spoke to him about the situation. We brokered a deal; I stooped down to his level, got his attention and asked him to look me straight in the eye. I told him that I knew he could do this performance. I told him that I would sit right in the front of the auditorium so that he could see me, and promised him that I would not stop looking straight at him, and if he kept his eyes on me and nothing else, he would get through this just fine. Somehow that worked, because he agreed to this plan. I'm sure he didn't feel that way, but it took a step of faith on Aaron's part to trust me and what we agreed to, because this sounded reasonable to Aaron.

We walked back upstairs and when it was Aaron's turn to perform, we never stopped looking at each other, and he did a great job… yes! The bigger success though, was that his faith in me grew, and he was not just acting in blind faith – to Aaron, this step of faith was reasonable.

There were other opportunities when raising our boys, but one that also sticks out to me was when, as a young teenager, he and I were on a mission's trip to Uganda, and the environment on one particular night appeared to be extremely dangerous;

especially for a young teenager's first experience of a foreign land, but we were able to complete a similar exercise of faith by reason producing trust.

It is this same type of faith that allows us to introduce Christ to our children throughout their lives. I have found that through His creation, we are able to introduce and strengthen our faith reasonably. Through creation and how God provides for us in many ways (fruits, vegetables, fish etc), the way we can enjoy nature and all of its benefits (swimming, fishing, travelling to distant places etc). When the boys would enjoy a great juicy watermelon or mango, it was not uncommon for us as parents to thank the Lord for such good food in front of them. Recognizing God, the creator, through the goodness of His creation, demonstrates how He is a good God for providing all of this, and also that He is an all-powerful God in creating everything. This fact can reasonably lead to the understanding as a child that if He is a good God, then I can trust Him in other things, hence building trust.

APPLICATION:

I. *How would you describe your faith — are you the blind faith believer or is your faith a reasonable faith based on the facts about who God is?*
II. *Discover as much as you can about God and His character through personal study (there's no race, He is patient).*

III. *Be deliberate about building your son or daughters faith in you, therefore producing trust – this is the natural process for having faith in a God we cannot see.*

IV. *Write down your faith building experiences.*

27

JESUS
– Meeting and understanding who Jesus is.

"This is the testimony in essence: God gave us eternal life; the life is in his Son. So, whoever has the Son, has life; whoever rejects the Son, rejects life."
Peterson, E. H. (2005). The Message: the Bible in contemporary language (1 Jn 5:11–12). Colorado Springs, CO: NavPress.

"Greater love hath no man than this, that a man lay down his life for his friends."

The Holy Bible: King James Version. (2009). (Electronic Edition of the 1900 Authorized Version., Jn 15:13). Bellingham, WA: Logos Research Systems, Inc.

The single most important thing any parent can do for their children is to introduce them to the person of Jesus Christ. To meet Jesus and accept him personally as Lord, is the ultimate expression of the familiar saying "friend for life"! As the verse preceding says, He gives us eternal life! This friend will always be there for you, never let you down and will always go to bat for you; in fact, this friend's love is pure and forever – that He gave his life for you. There is no greater love!

I remember regularly taking opportunities to talk about Jesus to my children, because regular talks about Him enabled them to get to know Him a little at a time. Different situations or events allowed me to talk specifically about His character, and what He represented. I am no scholar, but I know that my job is to let people know, especially my children, who Christ is. The great thing about Jesus, is that He comes knocking on everyone's door (their heart), and asks if they will trust Him with their lives, and He does the rest as they respond. We as parents are just the facilitators, the introducers, if you will.

I remember with fondness one starry night whilst driving home, and my middle son Brandon, began to cry as he was looking out of the window. When asked, he proceeded to proclaim how he loved Jesus because He could see Him in the stars! That was the result of the introduction – Jesus did the rest through His creation, and established a friend for life in Brandon!

APPLICATION:

I. Make it a priority to get to know Jesus if you haven't already done so – it is a continual process but it is ever so rewarding. Daily talks and reading of His word (Bible) will nurture your understanding and growth in Him.

II. *Look for and cherish opportunities to talk to your children about Jesus, just plain and simple. Talk about Him like you would your best friend. He is in fact a person, and not a religion or idea – He is Lord.*

28

WORLDVIEW
–How do we see the world

"But in your hearts set Christ apart as holy [and acknowledge Him] as Lord. Always be ready to give a logical defense to anyone who asks you to account for the hope that is in you, but do it courteously and respectfully." The Amplified Bible. (1987). (1 Pe 3:15). La Habra, CA: The Lockman Foundation.

'Everybody has a worldview… Your worldview generates the basic assumptions that you bring to the questions of life, to the decisions you make, to the opinions you form, and to the conclusions you draw.'

Worldview as a Concept - Andy Bannister, RZIM Academy Lecturer

Fairy Tales, Marvel comics, reality TV, are all components of our world today. I remember with great joy, going to movies with the boys like Spiderman, Transformers, Star Wars and Star Trek– that was awesome! And to this day, I've still got a movie buddy in Connor, who like me, is somewhat of a movie buff.

The media, particularly television and movies, continue to be the avenue through which Hollywood shapes our view on things. It is changing the way we see the world, our worldview. There used to be a time generally, when we could rely on the media to help us shape our children's world view, but that is no longer the case – we are absolutely on our own in that respect.

I remember some very interesting conversations with the boys about things we never spoke about when I was their age, and they were tough conversations about how we saw the world.

One of my favourite authors and apologist, Ravi Zacharias, Founder and President of Ravi Zacharias International Ministries (RZIM), has defined worldview through 4 questions around Origin, Meaning, Morality and Destiny:

"Origin- Where did I come from? What does it mean to be human?

Meaning- Is there purpose to life?

Morality – How should I live? Is there an objective right and wrong?

Destiny – Ultimately, where am I headed?"

I know you're thinking, this is deep Eugene, we're talking about parenting, not philosophy 101?

As parents helping our children to formulate the correct worldview, the sooner they will be able to navigate through life, making good decisions whilst operating within a sound understanding of right and wrong.

⚷ **APPLICATION:**

I. *Know what you believe (worldview), there's no point trying to develop worldview in your children when you don't know what you believe. Formulate your worldview based around the questions of Origin, Meaning, Morality and Destiny.*

II. *When parenting, as much as possible treat every situation individually and always look for opportunities to evaluate their decisions or conclusions. For instance, why we would take a mobile phone we found on the playground to the school office instead of keeping it for ourselves.*

29

PRAYER

–Establish the habit of conversational prayer

Be unceasing in prayer [praying perseveringly]; Thank [God] in everything [no matter what the circumstances may be, be thankful and give thanks], for this is the will of God for you [who are] in Christ Jesus [the Revealer and Mediator of that will].

The Amplified Bible. (1987). (1 Th 5:17–18). La Habra, CA: The Lockman Foundation.

Prayer – it's the word many are afraid of because they don't think they can pray, or they are shy to pray out loud. There are many reasons why people don't pray; for me growing up, it was only the super spiritual that prayed (usually little old ladies that had really loud voices, because you have to have a loud voice in order for God to hear you, and oh, it has to be at least 3-5 minutes long in order to be authentic!) But then, I learned that prayer is nothing more than talking to Triune God, and frankly, he hears what's in your heart and not what comes out of your mouth, because we all know we can say or learn anything to repeat that sounds good in prayer. Prayer is the most powerful tool disciples of Christ have in our arsenal, and that extends especially to our responsibility as parents. Prayer changes things, facilitates perspective, wisdom and protection. Prayer also is our most powerful weapon against the things we can't see, or when our children are not with us – we have prayer, they have prayer.

Parenting and praying go hand in hand as your little ones grow. Lorene and I prayed and continue to pray for ABC, daily together with thanksgiving, and I know separately when we think of them throughout the day. I can assure you they are not long drawn out prayers, they are quick and to the point because time is precious. We also prayed with the boys about anything that concerned them, whether it be Aaron who was terrified of playing his violin in front of a large crowd in his school uniform, or with Connor during his GCSE final exams space (every exam), we made prayer the norm for every situation.

We pray for everything, nothing is off limits when it comes to the boys. We pray for physical and mental wellbeing. We pray that they will find great jobs, just suited for them and who they are. We pray for their future spouse and children, we pray against attacks that would destroy them, and most importantly, we pray that they will grow and mature into strong; men of integrity, compassion, love and wisdom – that they will have close and personal relationship with the Lord, and be successful in God's eyes. They are that important, their lives depend on it.

🔑 APPLICATION

I.   *If you haven't already, practice talking to the Lord about everything you do, yes about everything, no matter how big or small. Establish the habit of conversational prayer with the Lord.*

II. *With God's help, make a list of the top 5 things that you want for your children and begin to daily pray for them.*

III. *If you haven't already, begin to pray with your children and establish early that prayer is not this special language only reserved the super religious.*

Printed in the United States
By Bookmasters